Joey

Story by Beverley Randell

Illustrated by Meredith Thomas

Mother Kangaroo had
a little gray baby called a joey.
He lived in her pouch.
He was warm and safe there,
and he had milk to drink.

Sometimes he put his head out
and looked around.

Weeks went by.
Joey was
getting big.
Sometimes he
came out of
the pouch and
had something
to eat.

But then
he jumped
back inside
the pouch,
head first.
He did not like
being out
for long.

One day Mother Kangaroo
put her head up
to smell the wind.
Some dogs were coming!

Off went all the kangaroos.
They had to get away
from the hungry dogs.

But Mother Kangaroo
had Joey in her pouch.
He was big and heavy,
and he slowed
her down.

Then Mother Kangaroo
saw some tall grass.
She made Joey fall into the grass
as she went past.

Off she went, faster and faster.
The dogs were
not going to catch her, now.

Joey hid in the tall grass.
He stayed very still.
The dogs did not see him
or smell him, so they ran past him.
For the first time,
Joey was all by himself,
and he did not like it.
Where was his mother?

It was night time,
and Joey wanted his mother.
He was very cold.

Thump . . . thump . . . thump . . .
Something was coming!

What was it?

It was Mother Kangaroo.
She had come back to find him.
Joey jumped into her pouch,
where he was
warm and safe
and happy
again.